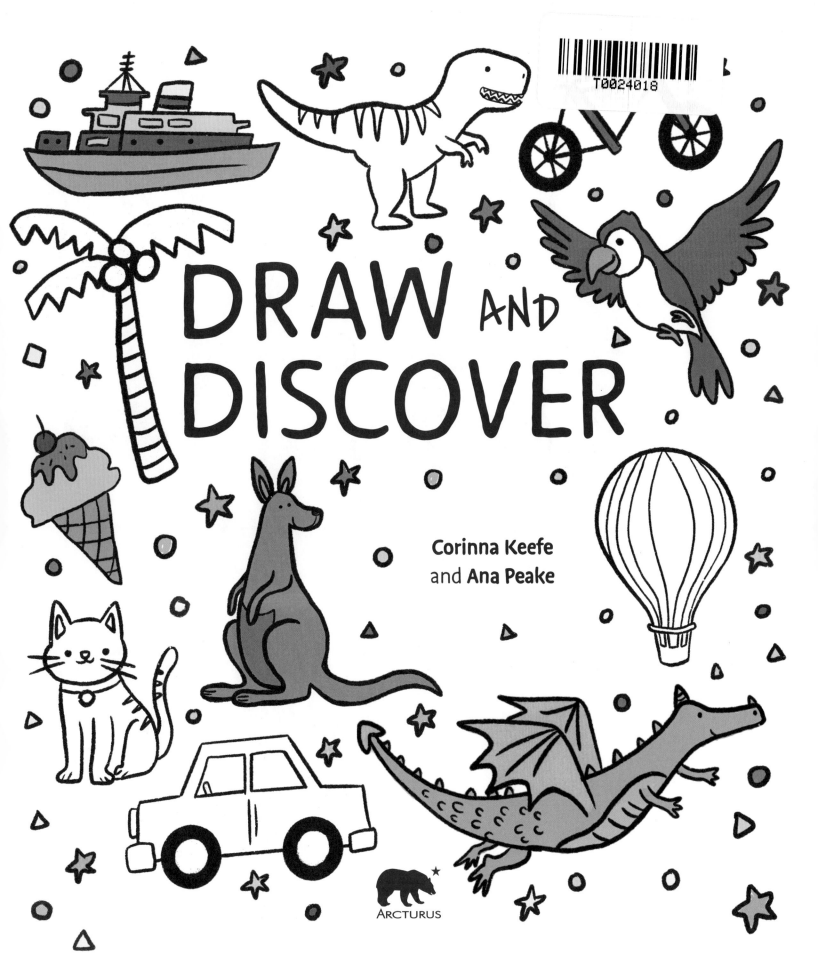

DRAW AND DISCOVER

Corinna Keefe
and **Ana Peake**

ARCTURUS

ARCTURUS

This edition published in 2024 by Arcturus Publishing Limited,
26/27 Bickels Yard, 151–153 Bermondsey Street, London SE1 3HA

Author: Corinna Keefe
Illustrator: Ana Peake
Editors: Violet Peto and Lucy Doncaster
Designer: Stefan Holliland
Managing Editor: Joe Harris

ISBN: 978-1-3988-3685-3
CH011060NT
Supplier 29, Date 1123, PI 00004294

Printed in China

How to Draw ...

How to Draw a Spacecraft

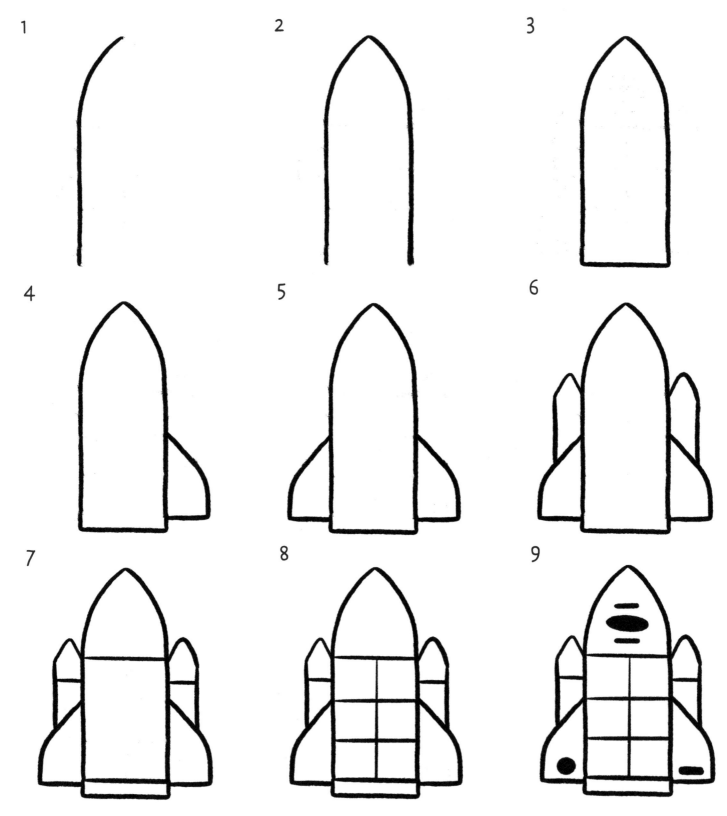

1

2

3

4

5

6

7

8

9

4

What does a spacecraft do?
It carries people and cargo into outer space and home again.

Liftoff!
A rocket is used to power spacecraft into space.

What next?
Once the rocket is the right distance from Earth, it releases the spacecraft.

All About Rockets

★ Rockets have to be very powerful to help spacecraft travel fast enough to reach space.

✶ The biggest rocket ever made was Saturn V. It took missions to the Moon and launched a space station.

How to Draw a Knight

1

2

3

4

5

6

7

8

9

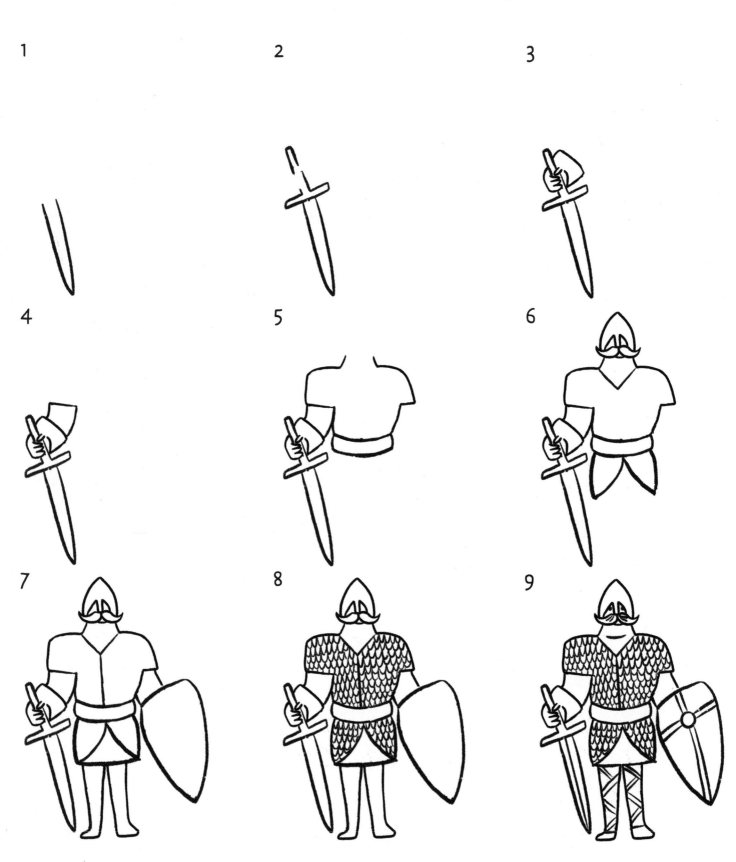

Norman who?
This knight is a Norman from the 11th century.

Heavy!
Chain mail shirts were made of hundreds of metal rings.

Crash! Clang!
The best swords were made of steel.

Shield skills
Knights could lock their shields together to make a wall.

All About Knights

* As well as swords, Norman fighters sometimes used battleaxes, crossbows, and spears.

7

How to Draw a Desert Island

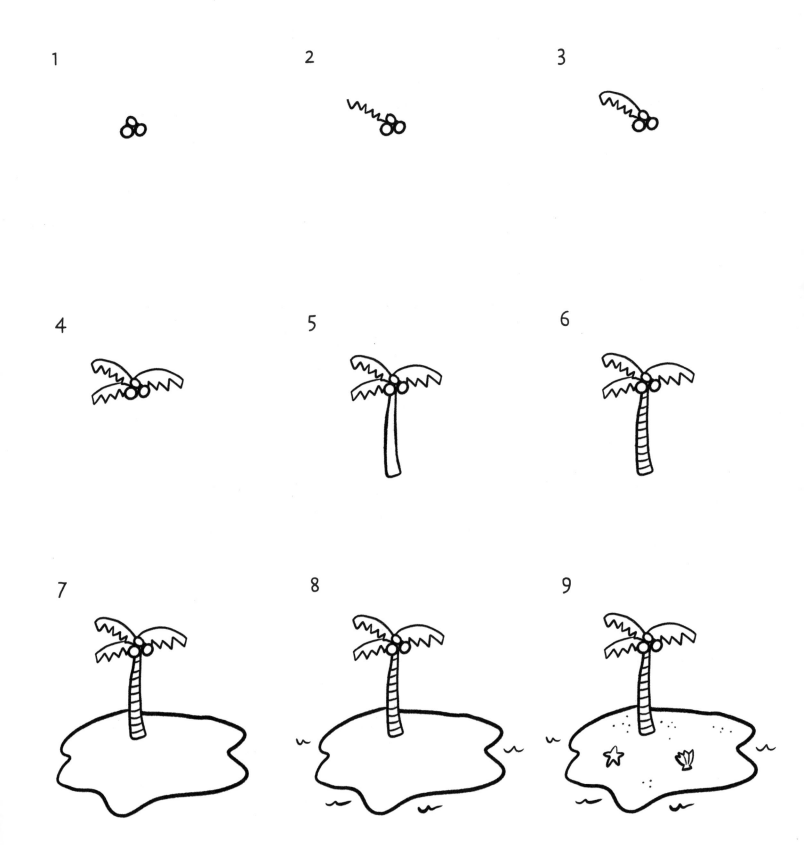

1

2

3

4

5

6

7

8

9

Sea snacks

Ancient explorers took coconuts on their journeys. Now, coconuts grow in warm places all over the world!

Plant giant

Coconut trees like this one can grow up to 30 m (100 ft) tall—that's about the same as six giraffes, one on top of the other!

Yum yum!

Coconuts contain water that is delicious to drink. The white part can be eaten or used to make coconut milk.

All About Desert Islands

★ A desert island is a place where no people live. This may be because there is no fresh water and not enough food.

How to Draw a Dragon

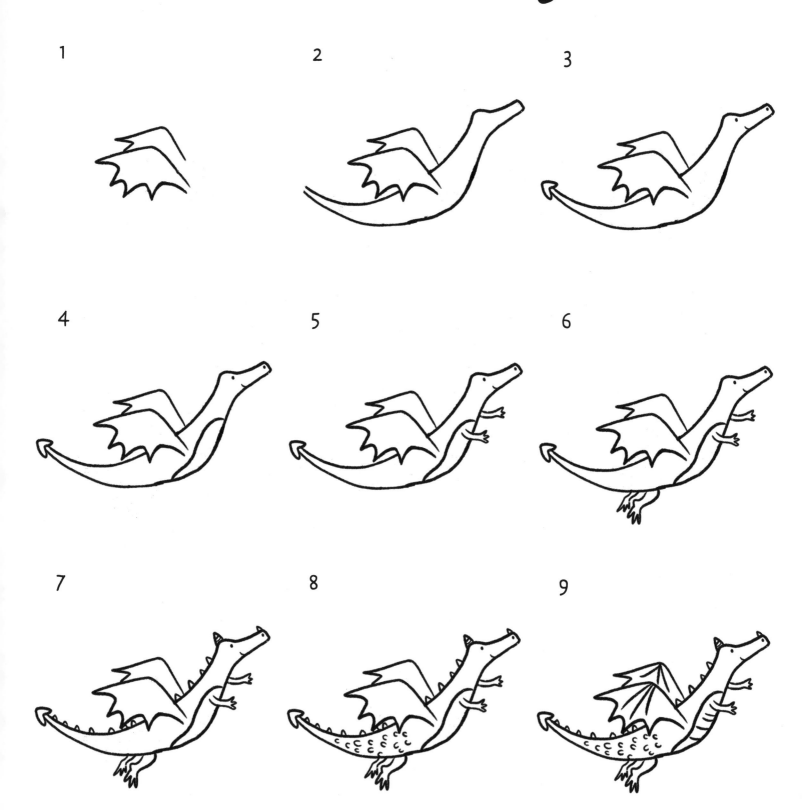

What's in a name?

The word *dragon* comes from the Greek word *drakon*, which means "big snake" or "sea creature."

Whoosh!

According to legend, dragons could blow flames at their enemies.

How many claws?

In Chinese legends, most dragons have three claws on each foot. Royal dragons have five!

All About Dragons

* There are stories about dragons all over the world. Some people think the legends are based on dinosaurs or crocodiles!

★ The Vikings believed that there was a dragon named Jörmungandr wrapped around the Earth.

How to Draw a Ferry

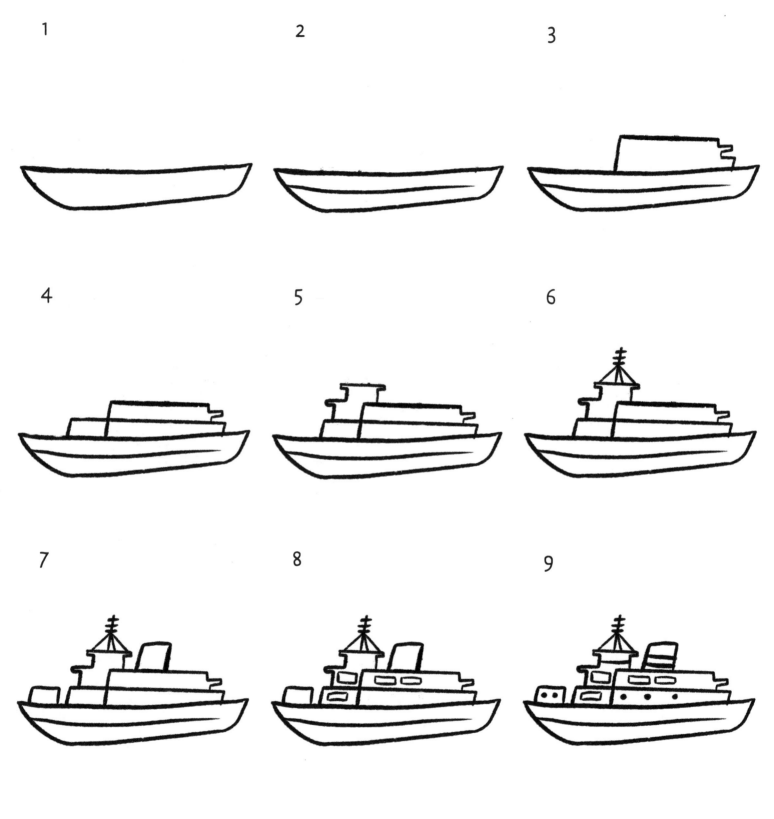

1

2

3

4

5

6

7

8

9

All About Ferries

* Ferries have been powered by rowing, sails, or engines. Now, electric batteries are starting to be used.

★ Vehicles travel in the lower part of the ship. People travel in the upper decks, where they can look out at the view.

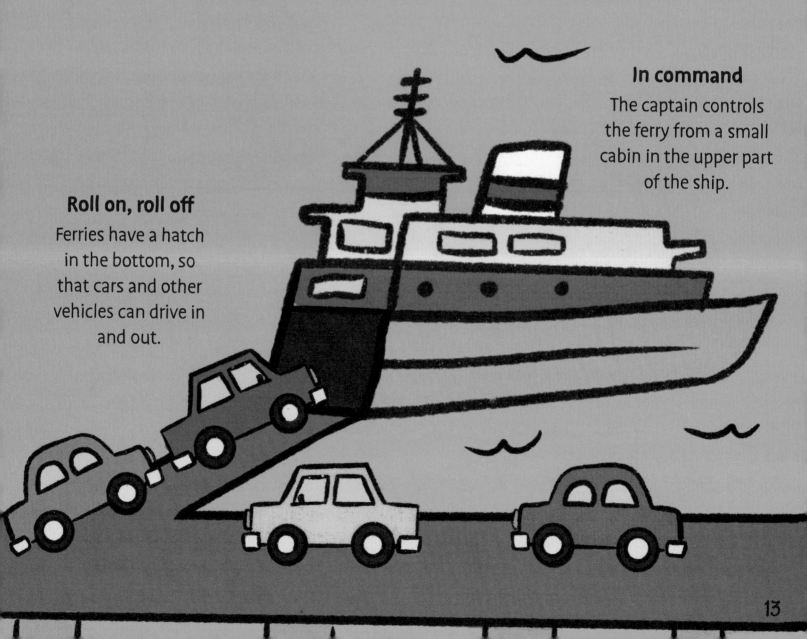

In command

The captain controls the ferry from a small cabin in the upper part of the ship.

Roll on, roll off

Ferries have a hatch in the bottom, so that cars and other vehicles can drive in and out.

How to Draw a Pterosaur

1

2

3

4

5

6

7

8

9

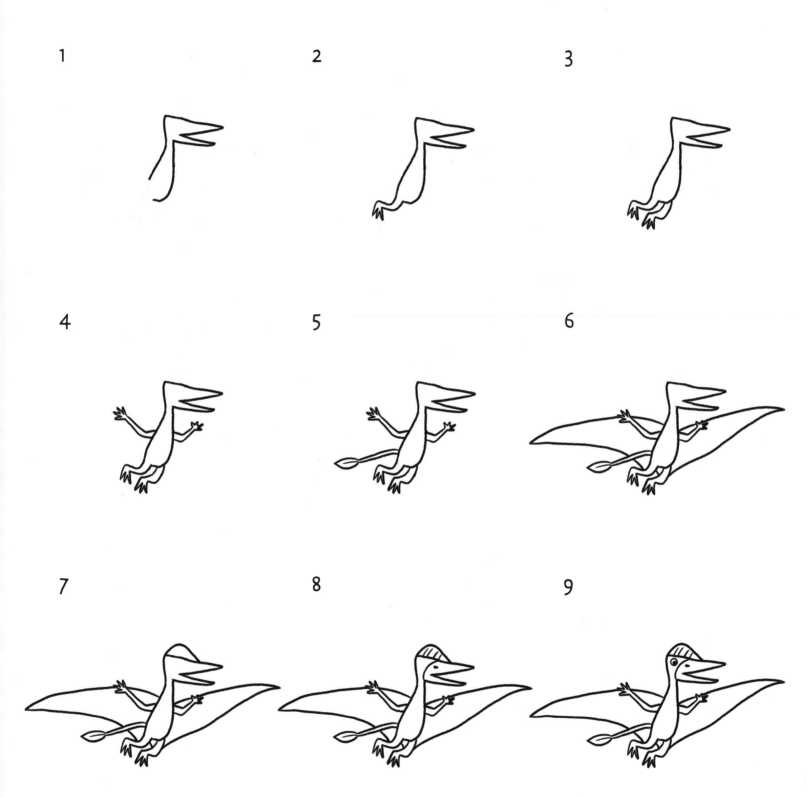

14

What's it for?

Pterosaurs had big, bony crests on their heads. These may have been used for showing off ... or maybe for steering in the air.

Zoom!

Pterosaurs could fly really fast with their strong wings.

Wrapped up warm

Pterosaurs had a coat of fur or feathers to keep them warm in the air.

All About Pterosaurs

★ Pterosaurs first appeared 228 million years ago. They are the largest flying animals that have ever existed.

★ Pterosaurs were the first vertebrates to take off and fly using their muscles, rather than just gliding in the air.

How to Draw a Bulldozer

1

2

3

4

5

6

7

8

9

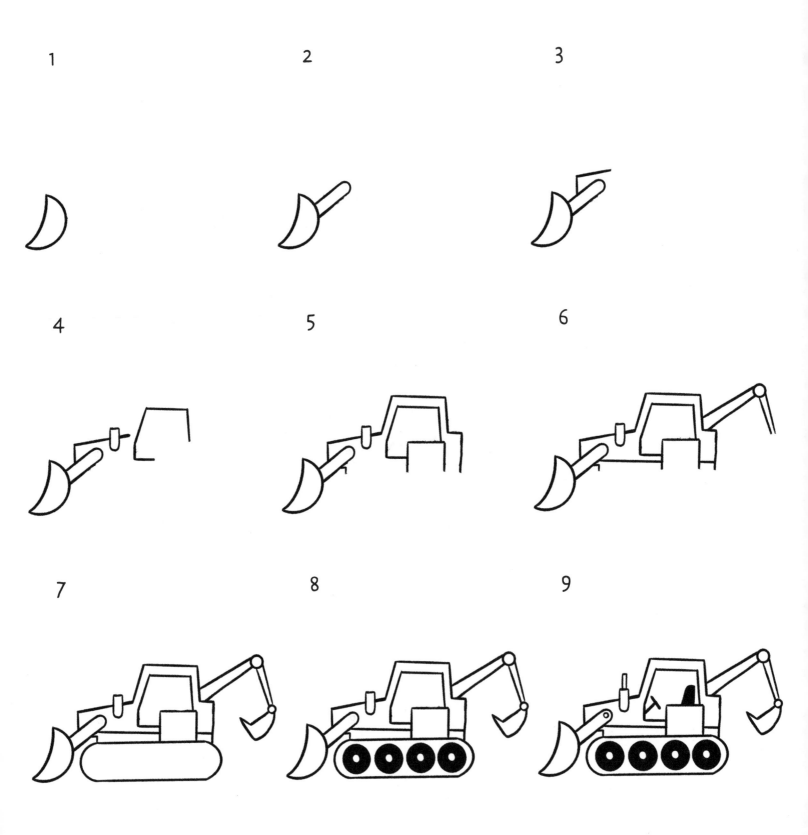

All About Bulldozers

★ The first bulldozer was invented in 1923. It was based on farm tractors, but with added tracks and more power.

A little help
The hook on the back of a bulldozer tears up the ground so it can be moved more easily.

Making tracks
Instead of wheels, bulldozers use special tracks to get over rough ground.

Anything goes
Bulldozers can push soil, sand, snow, rocks, and even trees with their front scoop.

How to Draw a Cat

1

2

3

4

5

6

7

8

9

All About Cats

* Cats can use their whiskers to feel air currents, measure small spaces, and even communicate!

★ Cats spend 70 percent of their lives sleeping. That's 16 hours a day!

Good listeners
Cats have cone-shaped ears to help them hear well.

Super smeller
A cat's sense of smell is about 14 times more powerful than a human's!

Night vision
Cats can see much better in the dark than humans can.

How to Draw a Cavewoman

1

2

3

4

5

6

7

8

9

All About Neanderthals

★ Neanderthals lived from at least 200,000 years ago up until about 35,000 years ago—when humans arrived.

Sharp minds
They used shaped and pointed stones as tools.

Ancient style
They probably wore simple clothes made from animal skins and fur.

Small but strong
Neanderthals were smaller than modern humans, but stronger.

How to Draw an Egyptian God

1

2

3

4

5

6

7

8

9

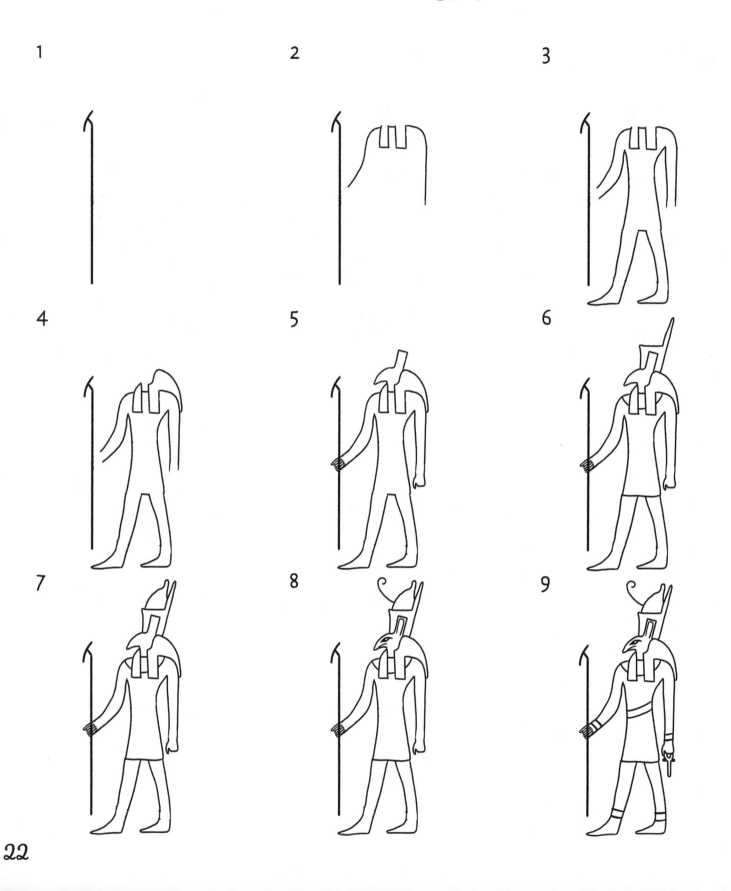

Bird's-eye view

Horus wore a double crown, like a pharaoh, to show that he ruled all of Egypt.

Who's Horus?

The Ancient Egyptians believed that Horus was the god of the sky, which is why he has a bird's head.

Lots of gods

The ancient Egyptians believed in many other gods and goddesses, too, including Ra, Isis, Osiris, and Amun.

All About Horus

★ Ancient Egyptians believed that the Sun and Moon were Horus's eyes. They used an eye as a symbol of his power.

✴ Every year, they celebrated Horus with a ceremony in which the King of Egypt had to fight a hippo!

How to Draw an Ice Cream Cone

1

2

3

4

5

6

7

8

9

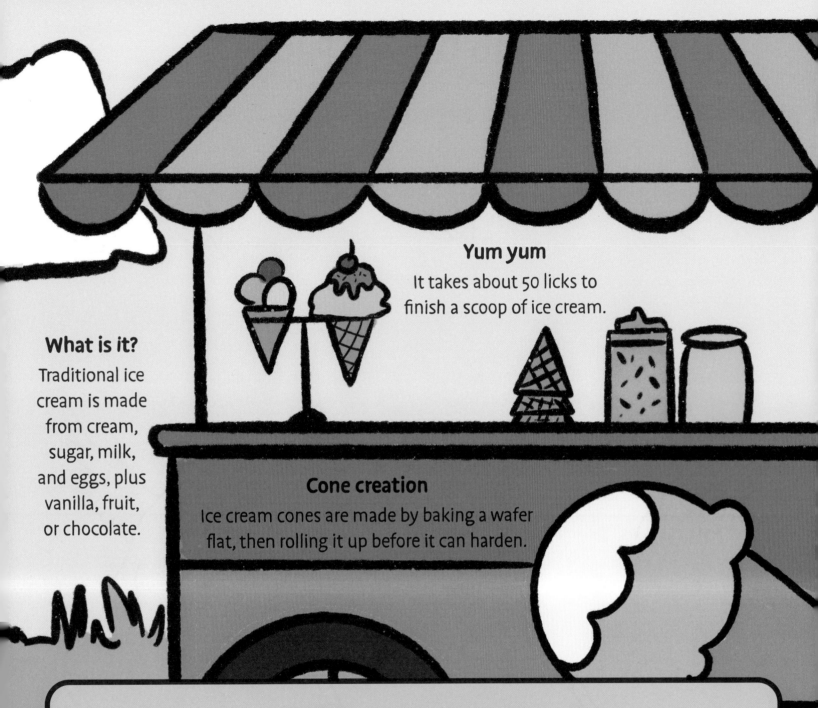

Yum yum
It takes about 50 licks to finish a scoop of ice cream.

What is it?
Traditional ice cream is made from cream, sugar, milk, and eggs, plus vanilla, fruit, or chocolate.

Cone creation
Ice cream cones are made by baking a wafer flat, then rolling it up before it can harden.

All About Ice Cream

✱ The most popular ice cream in the world is chocolate, followed by vanilla and mint chocolate chip.

★ Top tip: If you get brain freeze when you eat ice cream, try pressing your tongue against the top of your mouth. You'll soon warm up again!

25

How to Draw a Parrot

1

2

3

4

5

6

7

8

9

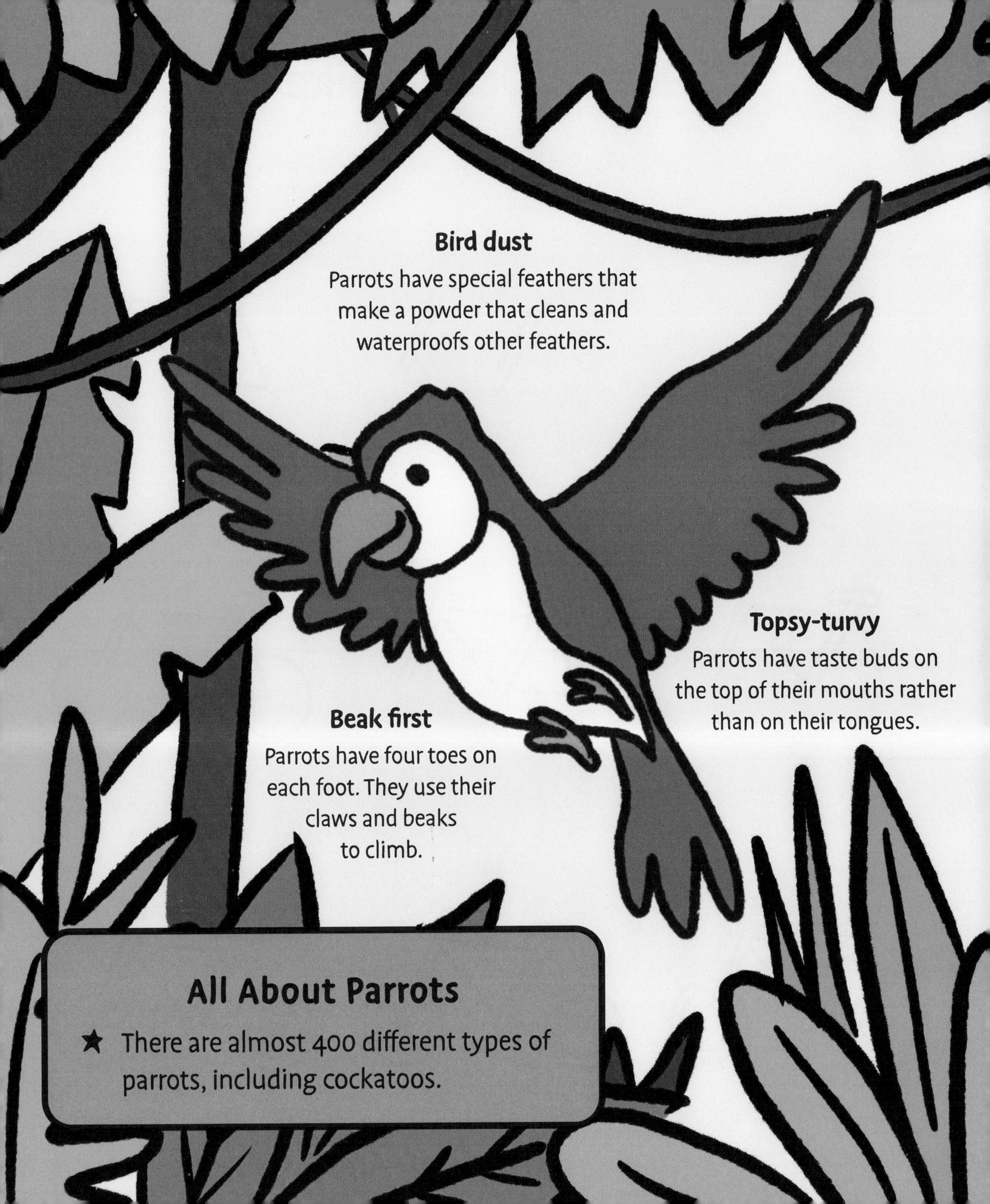

Bird dust

Parrots have special feathers that make a powder that cleans and waterproofs other feathers.

Topsy-turvy

Parrots have taste buds on the top of their mouths rather than on their tongues.

Beak first

Parrots have four toes on each foot. They use their claws and beaks to climb.

All About Parrots

★ There are almost 400 different types of parrots, including cockatoos.

How to Draw a Bike

1

2

3

4

5

6

7

8

9

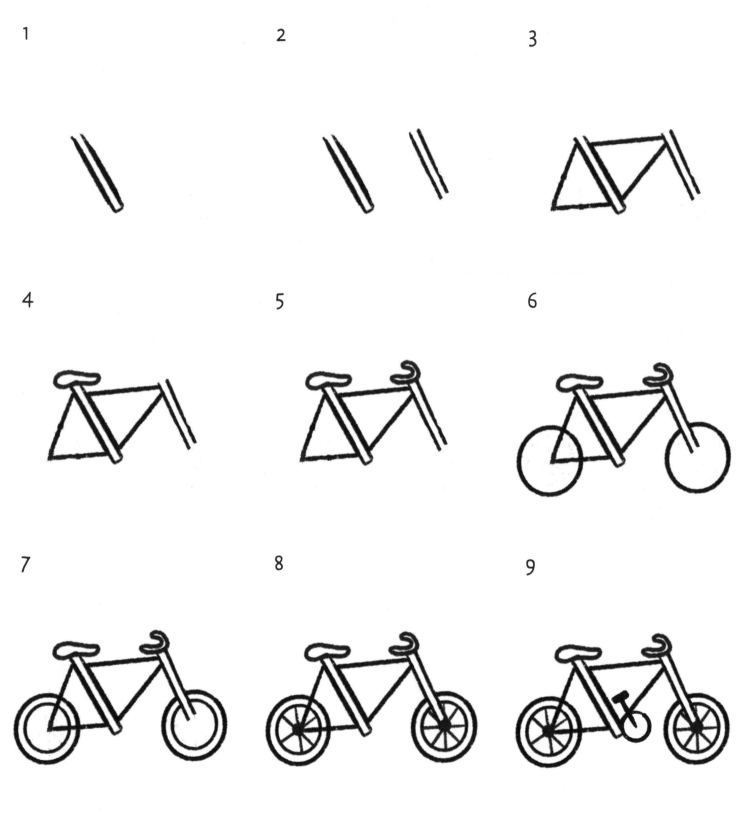

How does it work?

When you pedal a bike, the wheels spin so fast that the bike can't fall over.

Stop!

When you squeeze the brakes on the handlebars, the brake pads push against the wheels to slow them down.

All About Bikes

★ There are 1 billion bikes in the world. About half of them are in China!

✳ The wheels on a bike are the same size to help you balance. If one wheel is too big, it's harder to stay up!

How to Draw a Christmas Tree

1

2

3

4

5

6

7

8

9

Evergreen

We usually use fir, pine, or spruce trees as Christmas trees because they are green even in winter.

Twinkle, twinkle

The star on top of a Christmas tree is a reminder of the star that guided the Three Wise Men in the Nativity story.

All About Christmas Trees

★ Almost all Christmas trees are grown on special farms rather than being harvested from the wild.

Brightly shining

Strands of light bulbs were first used as decorations in 1880.

How to Draw a Skeleton

1

2

3

4

5

6

7

8

9

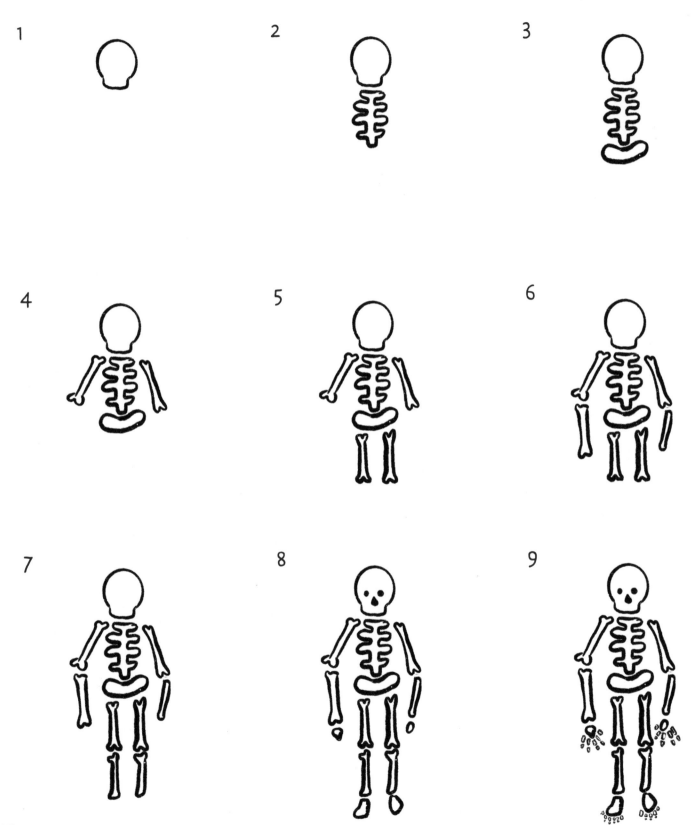

All About Skeletons

* Babies are born with 270 bones—more than an adult! As they grow, some of these bones join together.

* The bone that supports your tongue is the only one that isn't connected to any others.

Tough teeth
Your teeth are even stronger than your bones!

How many?
Adult human skeletons have 206 bones.

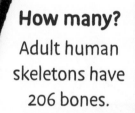

Long legs
The thigh bone is the longest bone in the human body.

How to Draw a Volcano

1

2

3

4

5

6

7

8

9

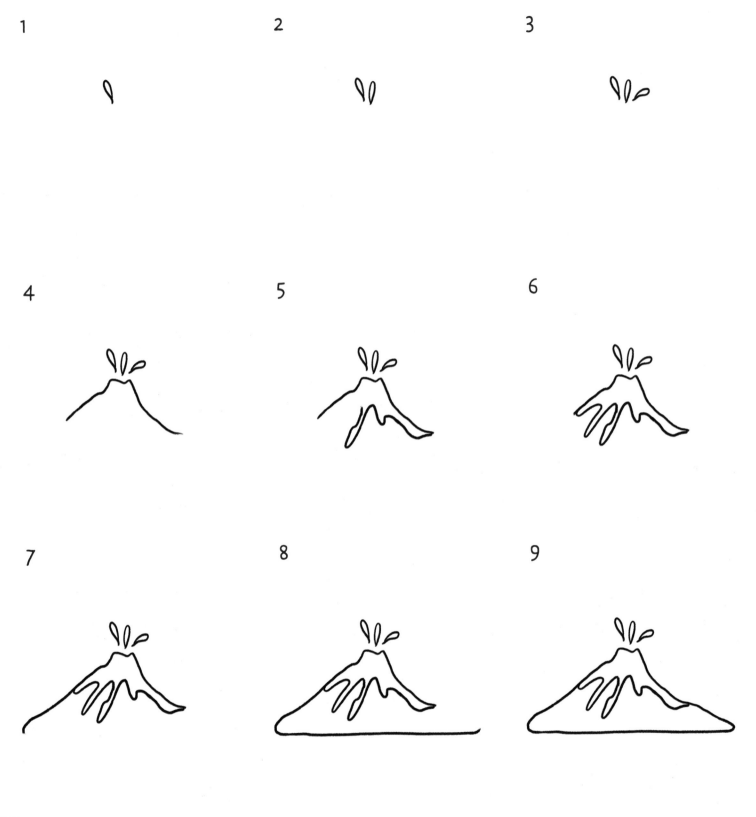

34

Boom!
When volcanoes erupt, they spit out gas, lava, and small pieces of rock.

Red hot!
Lava can be up to 1,250 °C (2,282 °F). That's hot enough to melt iron!

What's the difference?
When super-hot liquid rock is still inside a volcano, it's called magma. When it spills out, it's called lava.

All About Volcanoes
★ There are more than 1,500 active volcanoes on Earth.

✳ Most volcanoes are underwater. When they erupt, they can create islands.

How to Draw a Hippo

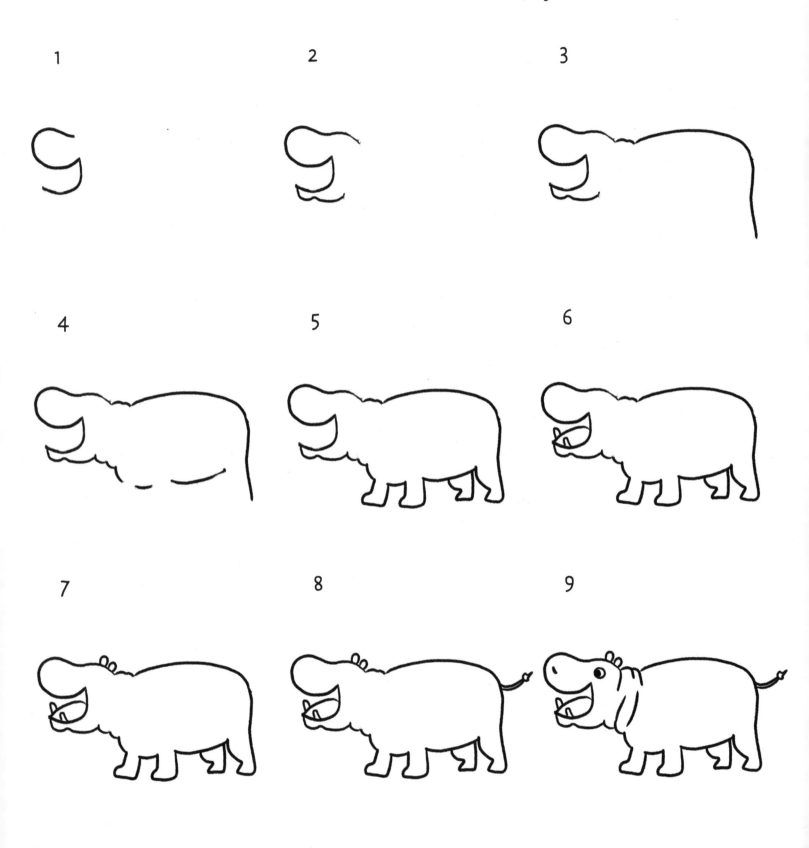

1

2

3

4

5

6

7

8

9

36

Sun safe

Hippos have red sweat! This protects them from sunburn.

Heavyweight

An adult hippo weighs almost as much as a small car.

Open wide

When a hippo opens its mouth as wide it will go, it can measure 120 cm (4 ft). This is enough space for a toddler to stand up in!

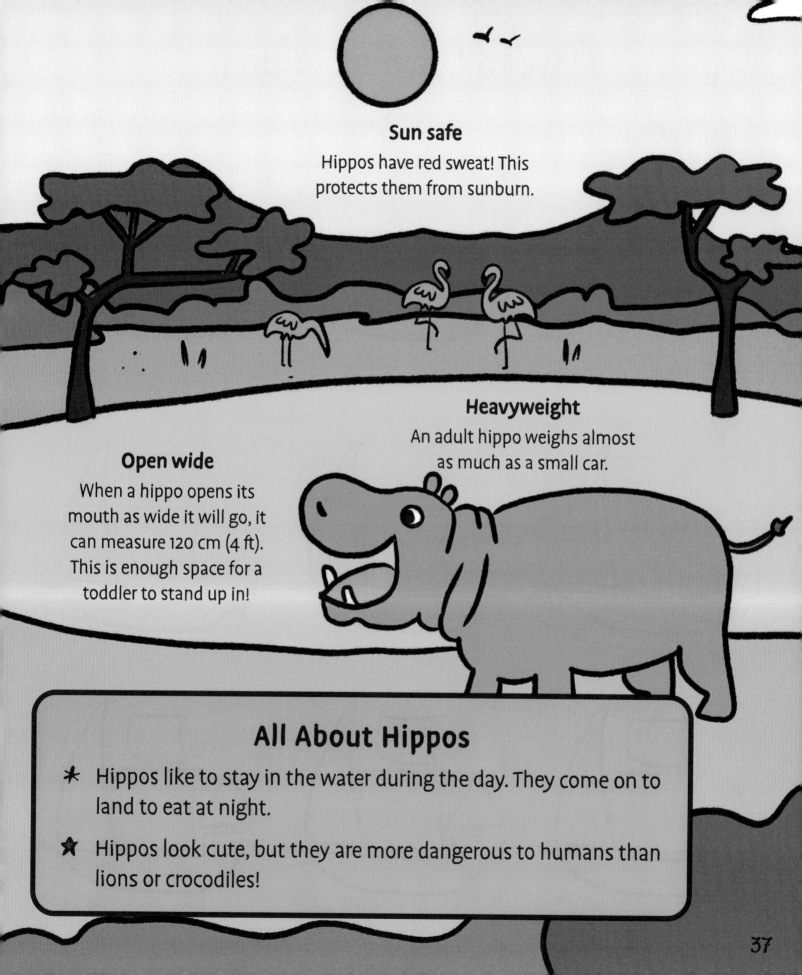

All About Hippos

* Hippos like to stay in the water during the day. They come on to land to eat at night.

* Hippos look cute, but they are more dangerous to humans than lions or crocodiles!

How to Draw a Sailboat

1

2

3

4

5

6

7

8

9

What are they?

Sailboats are ships with sails. These pieces of cloth are attached to poles called masts. The wind gets caught in the sails and pushes the sailboat along.

Double trouble

Having two masts makes this type of ship fast and easy to sail.

All About Sailboats

★ Sailboats come in lots of different sizes. Large ones can be used to cross huge oceans using just the power of the wind.

★ Boats are used to carry people and cargo all over the world. They have also been used to explore and discover new places.

How to Draw a Tiger

1

2

3

4

5

6

7

8

9

40

Night vision

In daylight, tigers can see as well as humans. At night, their vision is six times better than ours!

Hide-and-seek

Every tiger has its own unique pattern of stripes to help it hide in the forest.

Watch out!

Tigers have long, sharp teeth and claws for catching and eating prey.

All About Tigers

★ Tigers are really good at swimming.

★ Tigers are amazing hunters. They hunt alone and at night, using their cat vision to find their prey.

How to Draw a Robot

1

2

3

4

5

6

7

8

9

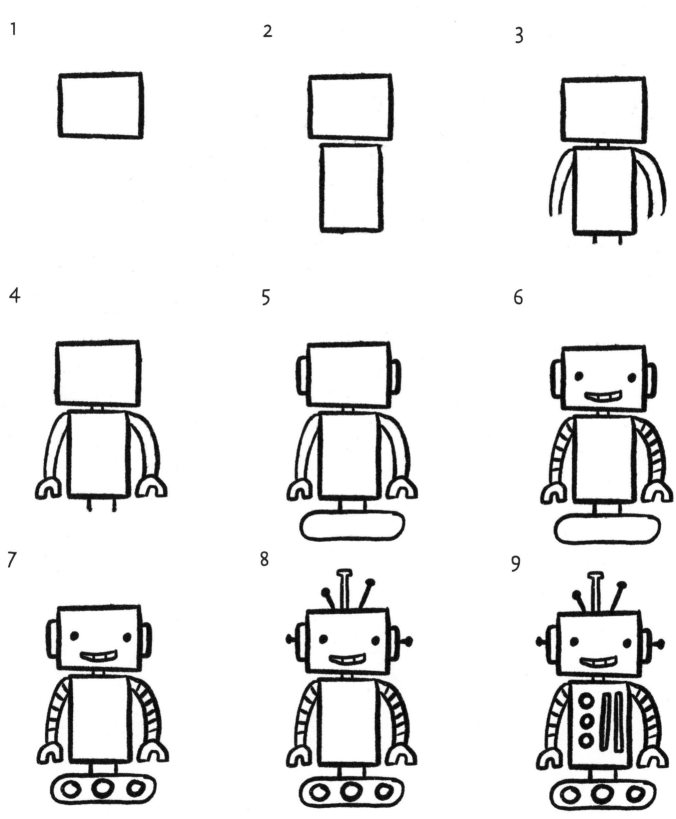

42

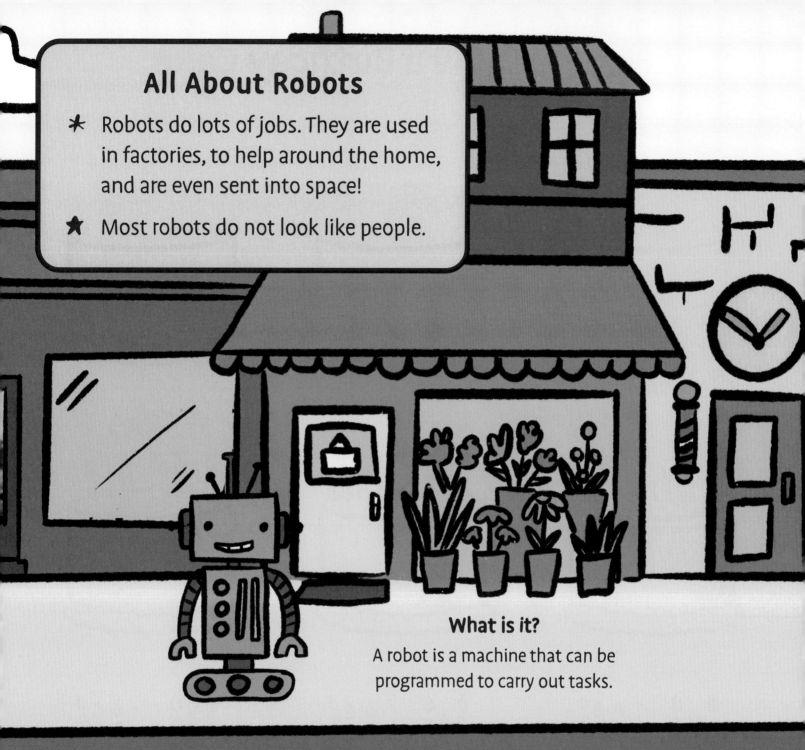

All About Robots

* Robots do lots of jobs. They are used in factories, to help around the home, and are even sent into space!

★ Most robots do not look like people.

What is it?
A robot is a machine that can be programmed to carry out tasks.

Look-alike
Robots that work with people are often designed to look like friendly humans, with a face, arms, and legs.

Learning to walk
It's hard to design a robot that can walk, run, and jump as well as a human. Some robots just have wheels instead.

How to Draw a Birthday Cake

1

2

3

4

5

6

7

8

9

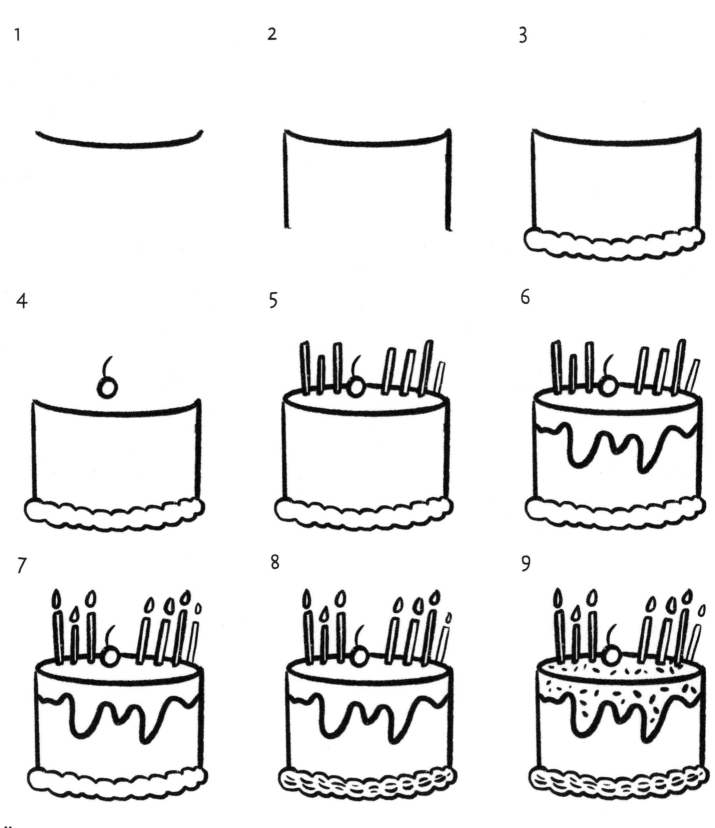

All rise

A cake is usually made with butter, sugar, flour, and eggs.

Let's celebrate!

Birthday cakes often have several layers and may be decorated with bright icing, candles, sprinkles, or other fancy decorations.

All About Birthday Cakes

★ The largest birthday cake ever was made in 1989 to celebrate the 100th birthday of a city in the United States.

★ The oldest person ever was a French woman who lived to be 122 years old. That's a lot of candles!

How to Draw a Castle

1

2

3

4

5

6

7

8

9

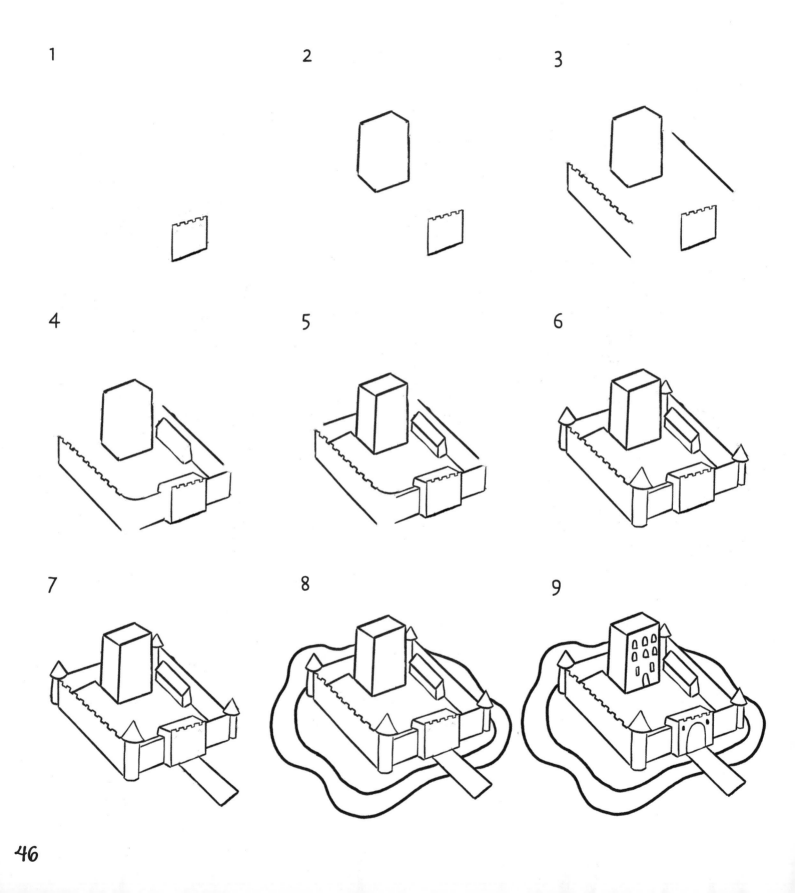

46

Everyone in!

In times of war, people living near a castle could often come and shelter inside.

Keeping safe

The central building of the castle is where the ruler lived. This was the safest place in the castle.

Bridging the gap

There is a ring of water called a moat around this castle. The moat could be crossed using a drawbridge.

All About Castles

★ Castles are strong buildings that were used to defend against enemies. They were often the homes of noble families.

How to Draw an Apple Tree

1

2

3

4

5

6

7

8

9

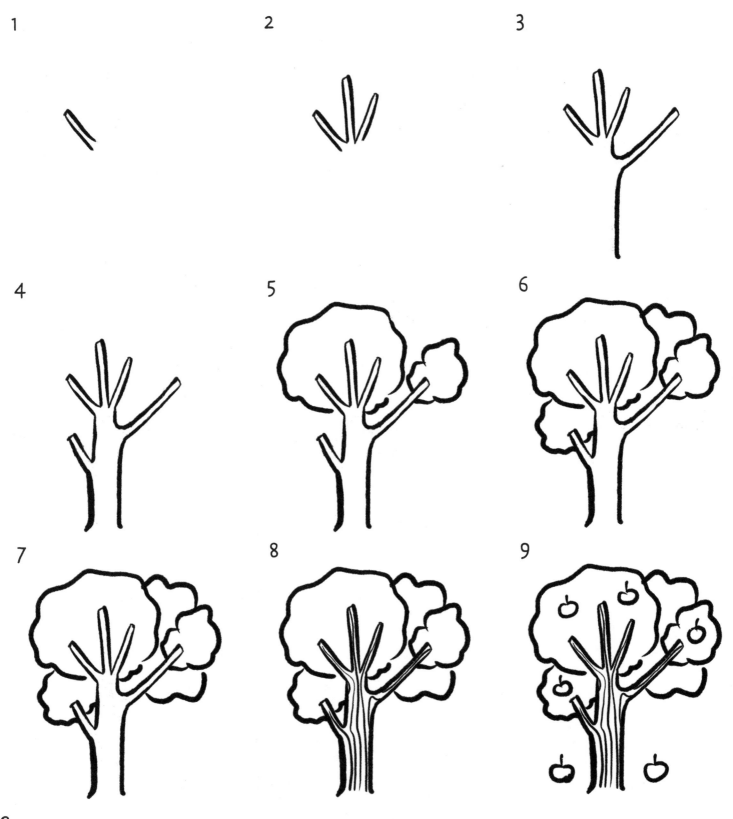

All About Apples

★ There are more than 7,500 different types of apples.

✳ Apples are a symbol of wisdom in many cultures. That's why they're often given as a gift to teachers!

What to look for

Apple trees have dark green, oval leaves with zigzag edges. If you feel underneath, they're furry, too!

Fruit and flowers

Apple trees have pink and white flowers, which develop into fruit.

Wait for it ...

Apple trees don't grow fruit until they are at least five years old.

49

How to Draw an Astronaut

1

2

3

4

5

6

7

8

9

Deep breath ...

An astronaut's backpack is full of air so they can breathe in space.

Whoosh!

In an emergency, the suit has a jetpack to help astronauts get back to the space station.

That's cool!

Astronauts wear another suit underneath, which has tubes of water in it to help them stay cool.

All About Astronauts

★ *Astronaut* comes from a Greek word meaning "star sailor."

✳ Spacesuits are like small spacecraft. They even have fans and electrical systems inside!

How to Draw a T. rex

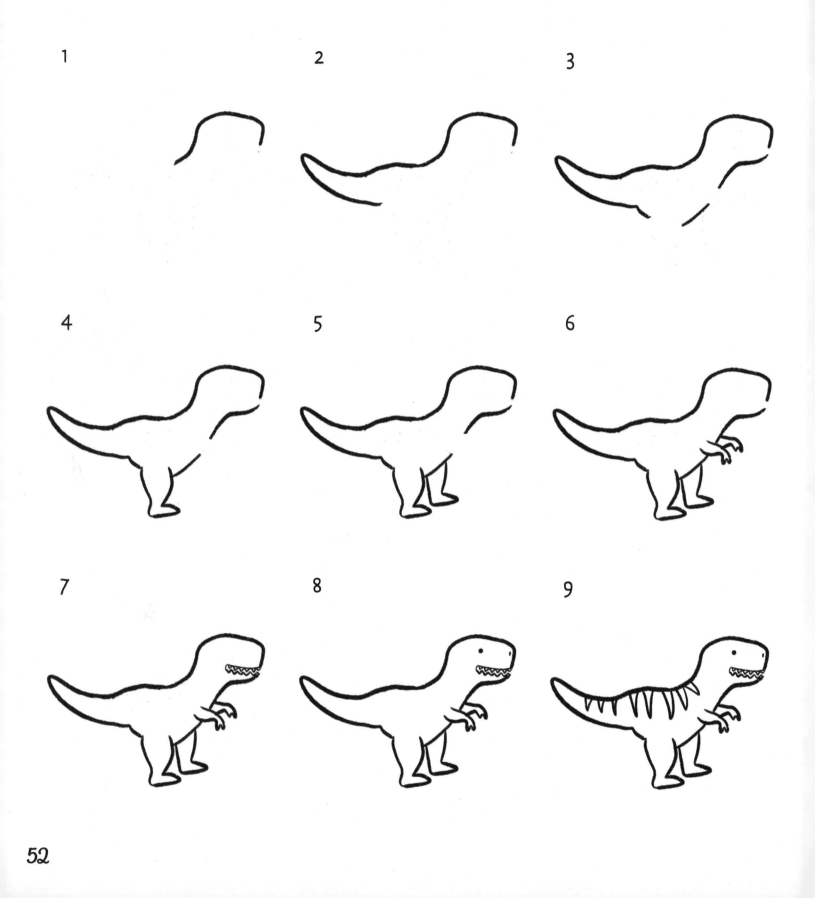

1

2

3

4

5

6

7

8

9

52

Quick thinker

T. rex had the largest brain of any meat-eater of its size.

Gulp!

T. rex didn't chew— it swallowed its food whole!

Tail-blazer

T. rex's large tail helped it to balance as it ran fast.

Handy!

T. rex's tiny, clawed arms were useful for holding prey close.

All About T. rex

✳ *Tyrannosaurus rex* lived about 90 to 66 million years ago. A fierce meat-eater, it was taller than two human adults standing on each other's shoulders.

★ *T. rex* is famous for its large, sharp teeth. In fact, the longest dinosaur tooth ever discovered was from a *T. rex*.

How to Draw a Car

1

2

3

4

5

6

7

8

9

All About Cars

★ The first cars were made around 1900. They didn't look much like modern cars and had very big wheels.

★ The fastest car ever is the Thrust SSC. In 1997, it reached 1,228 km/h (763 mph)—faster than the speed of sound!

Wheely different

Cars come in many shapes and sizes. Some have three wheels!

Lights up

Special lights tell people when cars are turning or slowing down.

How to Draw a Scuba Diver

1

2

3

4

5

6

7

8

9

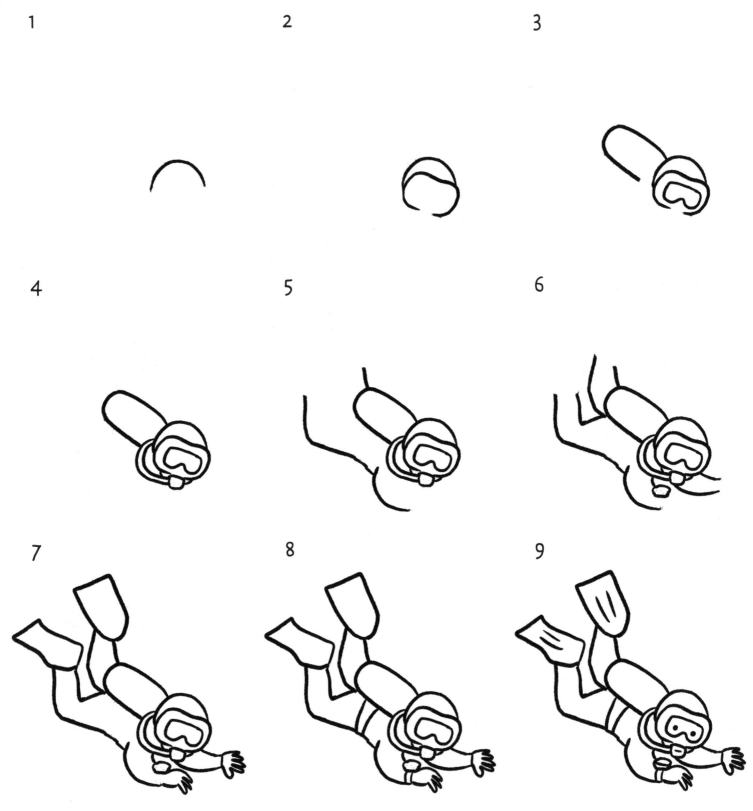

Flip-flop
Scuba divers wear fins
to help them move
through the water.

In and out
Divers breathe in
air from the tanks
on their back and
breathe out bubbles.

Snug!
Scuba divers usually wear
special suits to keep them
warm and comfortable.

All About Scuba Diving

* *Scuba* stands for "Self-Contained Underwater Breathing Apparatus."

* The longest scuba dive lasted for 212 hours!

How to Draw a Bowl of Noodles

1

2

3

4

5

6

7

8

9

Stre-e-e-tch!

Noodles are made by rolling or stretching dough into long strips. They can be cut or twisted into lots of different shapes.

Bubble, bubble

Noodles are cooked in boiling water to make them soft, stretchy, and tasty.

Wow!

People have used chopsticks to eat for over 3,000 years.

All About Noodles

✱ Noodles were probably invented in China. They are now eaten all over the world.

★ There are 310 different types of pasta noodles in Italy, with more than 1,300 names.

How to Draw an Ancient Monument

1

2

3

4

5

6

7

8

9

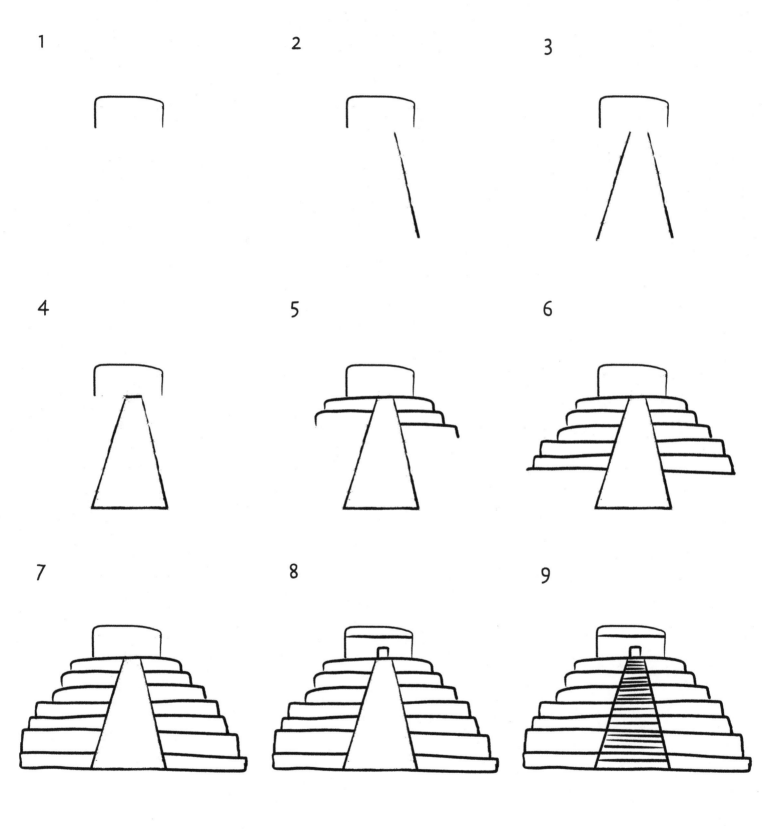

Stacking blocks

Sometimes, step pyramids like this one were built on top of other pyramids—stacking them higher and higher!

Pointed or flat?

Step pyramids are different from Egyptian pyramids because they have flat tops.

Solid stone

Most step pyramids are made from stone blocks, but they can also be made from clay or earth.

All About Step Pyramids

★ People have built step pyramids all over the world. They are huge, impressive buildings that can last for hundreds of years.

★ The largest step pyramid is Tlachihualtepetl (*Tlah-chee-wahl-teh-peh-tl*) in Mexico. Its name means "mountain made by hand."

How to Draw a Cactus

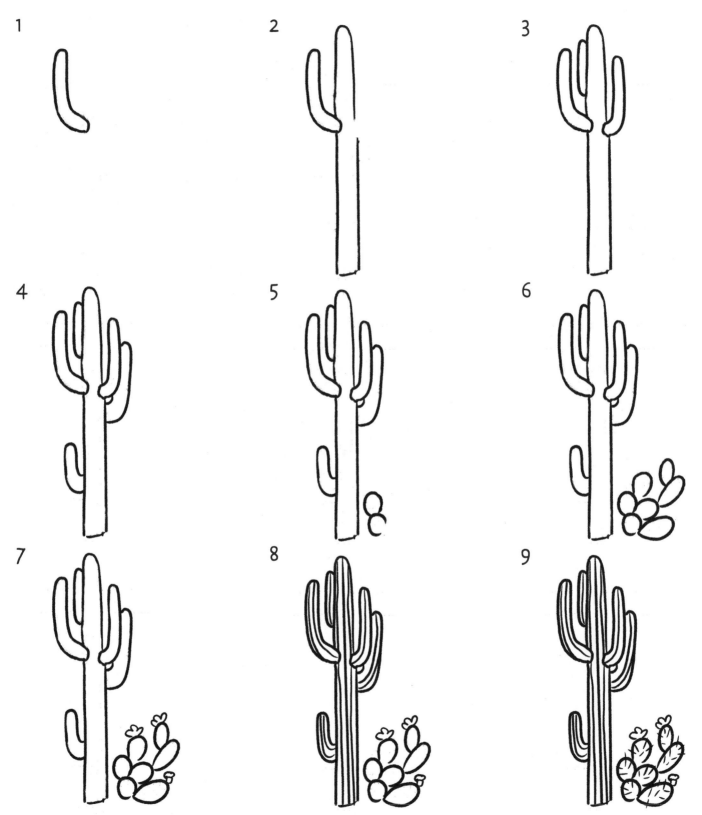

1

2

3

4

5

6

7

8

9

Classic cactus

The tallest cactus found in the United States is the saguaro cactus, like this one.

Wow!
A cactus can live for up to 200 years.

Thirsty?
A cactus is designed to store water. It has thick, fleshy stems and spines instead of leaves.

All About Cacti

✱ There are about 2,000 different types of cacti. They are found all over the world.

✱ Cacti are very useful. Some of them can be used for food, fuel, medicine, and even making needles and combs!

How to Draw a Wizard

1

2

3

4

5

6

7

8

9

Magic hats

Pointed, golden hats from the Bronze Age have been found in Europe. Did they belong to ancient wizards?

Wands of power

Witches and wizards are usually shown using wands to cast their spells.

What does it mean?

Wizard is an old English word that means "wise man." *Witch* means a woman who can do magic or see into the future.

All About Wizards

★ The Harry Potter stories about a young English wizard are the bestselling book series in history.

How to Draw a Kangaroo

1

2

3

4

5

6

7

8

9

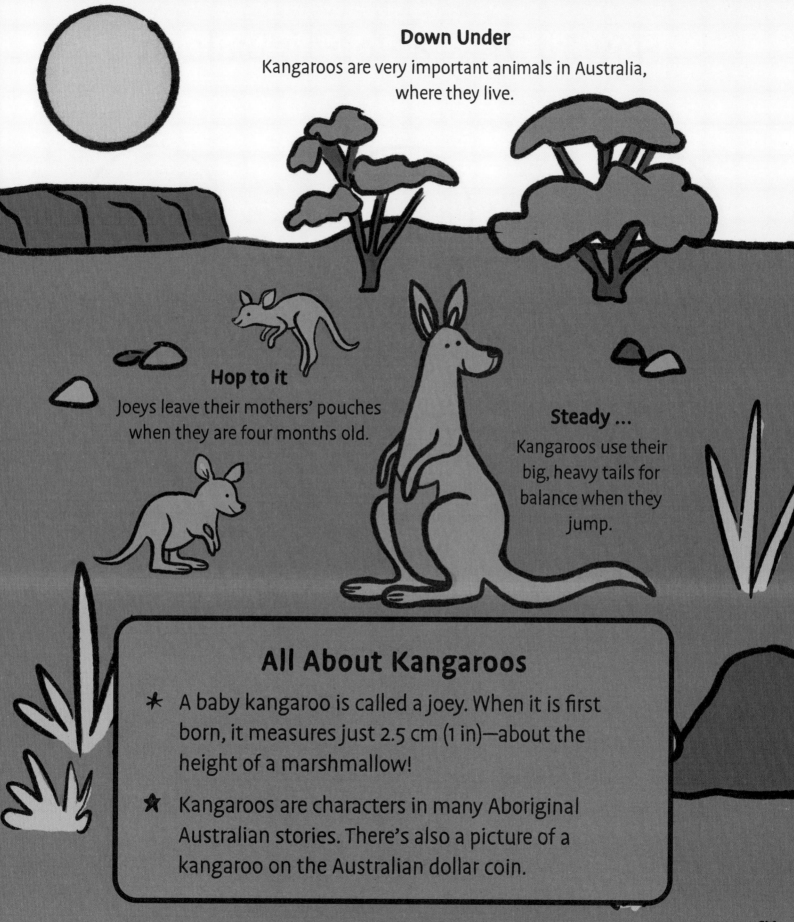

Down Under

Kangaroos are very important animals in Australia, where they live.

Hop to it

Joeys leave their mothers' pouches when they are four months old.

Steady ...

Kangaroos use their big, heavy tails for balance when they jump.

All About Kangaroos

* A baby kangaroo is called a joey. When it is first born, it measures just 2.5 cm (1 in)—about the height of a marshmallow!

⭐ Kangaroos are characters in many Aboriginal Australian stories. There's also a picture of a kangaroo on the Australian dollar coin.

How to Draw a Hot-Air Balloon

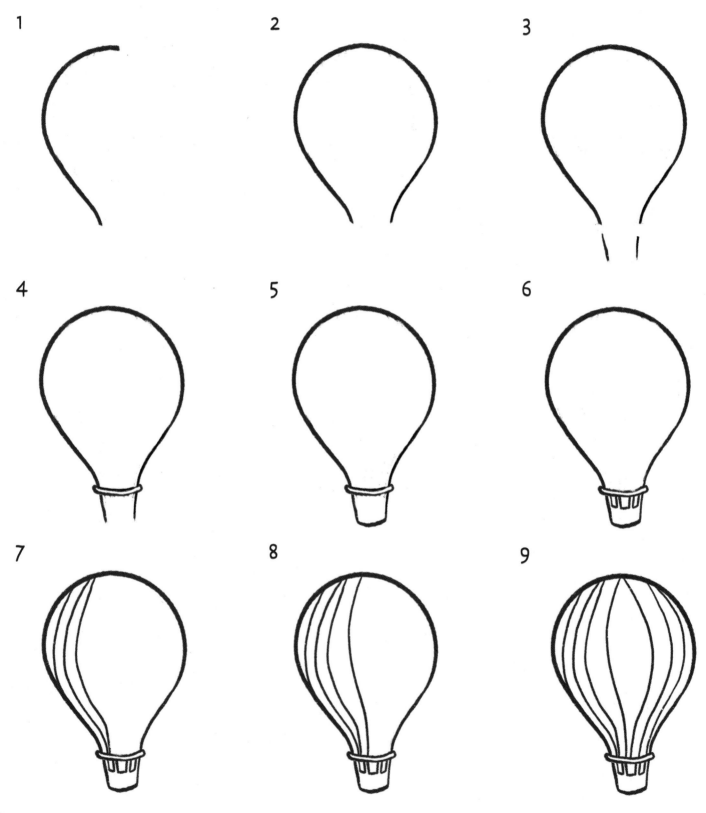

1

2

3

4

5

6

7

8

9

Hotting up

The balloon is full of hot air. The hot air is lighter than the cold air outside, so it rises up.

Taken for a ride

The basket underneath the balloon is where people stand.

How to land

To slow the balloon down or come back down to earth, the pilot lets hot air out of the top of the balloon.

All About Hot-Air Balloons

★ The first hot-air balloon was built by two brothers, Joseph-Michel and Jacques-Étienne Montgolfier.

★ In 1991, a hot-air balloon flew over 7,000 km (4,700 miles) ... all the way from Japan to Canada!

How to Draw a Wheelchair

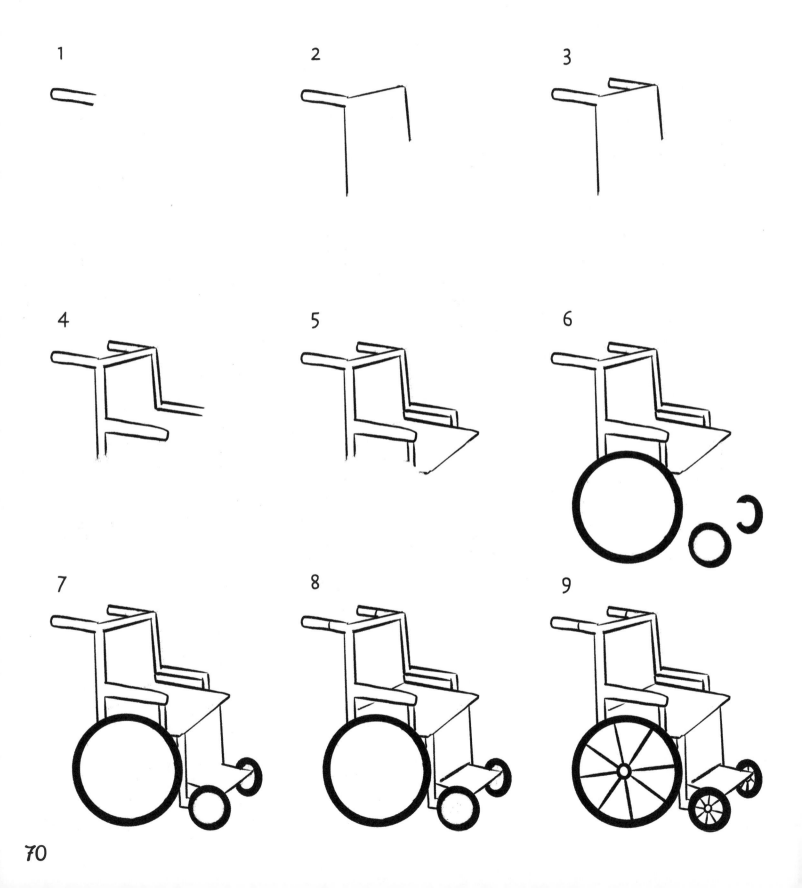

1

2

3

4

5

6

7

8

9

70

All About Wheelchairs

★ People have used wheelchairs for hundreds of years—since at least 500 BCE!

✳ 3.3 million people in the United States are wheelchair users.

Sitting comfortably
The footrest on the wheelchair helps with sitting up straight.

Manual or power?
Some wheelchairs, called powerchairs, have an electric motor to move the wheels along.

Go faster!
A self-propelled wheelchair like this one has large back wheels, so it's easier for the user to push themselves along.

How to Draw a Pirate

1

2

3

4

5

6

7

8

9

Pieces of eight

According to the Pirate Code, if a pirate lost their leg, they got 800 silver coins.

Slash! Stab!

Pirates often used a curved sword called a cutlass to fight their enemies.

Undercover

Anne Bonny and Mary Read were famous female pirates operating in the Carribean aboard the *William*.

All About Pirates

★ The "Golden Age" of pirates was from 1650 to 1720.

★ The famous skull-and-crossbones flag of the pirates is called the Jolly Roger.

How to Draw a Piano

1

2

3

4

5

6

7

8

9

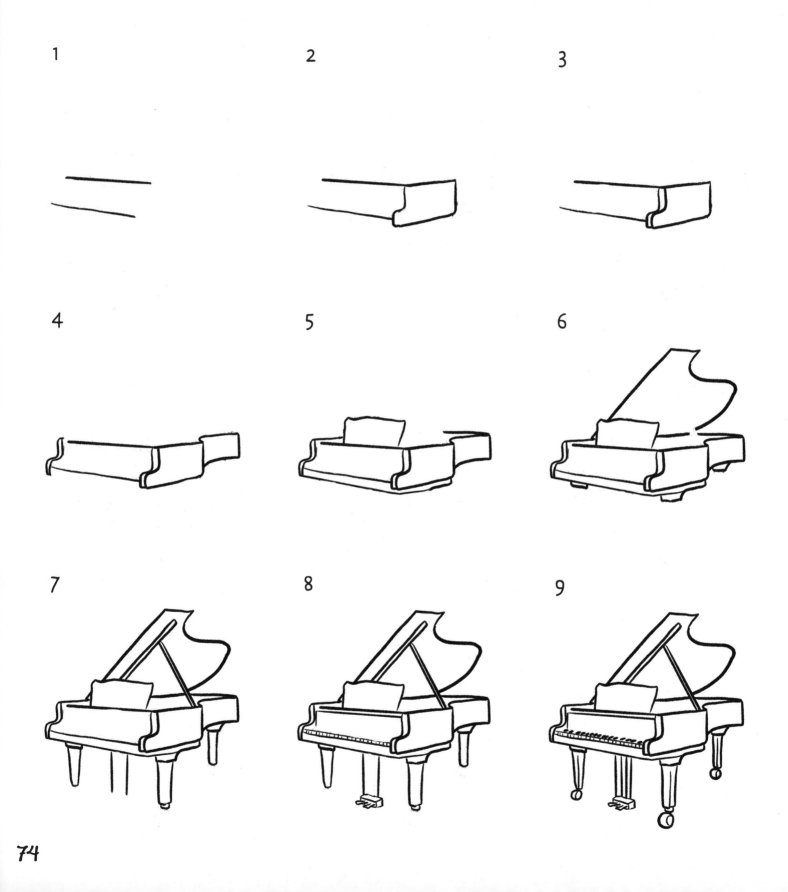

74

All About Pianos

★ The first piano was invented in Italy, around 1700.

✳ A grand piano like this one has 88 keys: 52 white keys and 36 black keys.

That's grand

A big, open-top piano like this is called a grand piano.

How it works

Each key controls a hammer inside the piano. The hammer hits a string to make a sound.

Shhh!

A pianist can use the pedals to make the piano quieter or hold notes for longer.

How to Draw a Stag Beetle

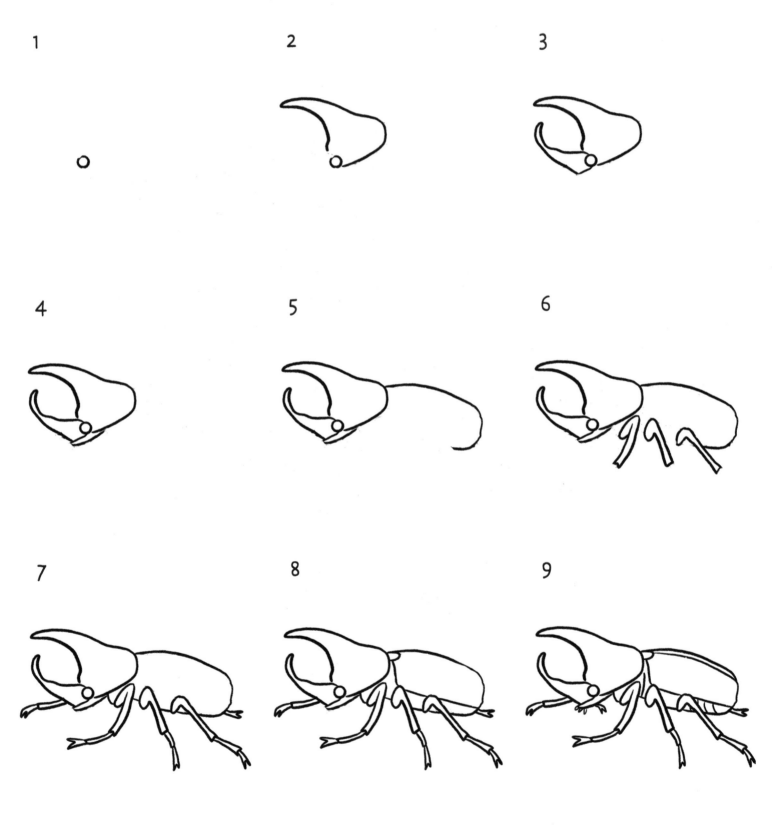

All About Stag Beetles

★ In Japan, some people keep stag beetles as pets.

★ It takes up to six years for a baby larva to develop into an adult stag beetle.

The insect with antlers

Stag beetles have six legs and two front "antlers," which they use to eat and fight with.

Liquids only

Adult stag beetles can't eat solid food. They drink tree sap and fruit juices.

Where?

Stag beetles like to live in oak forests, where they lay their eggs in rotting wood.

How to Draw a Submarine

1

2

3

4

5

6

7

8

9

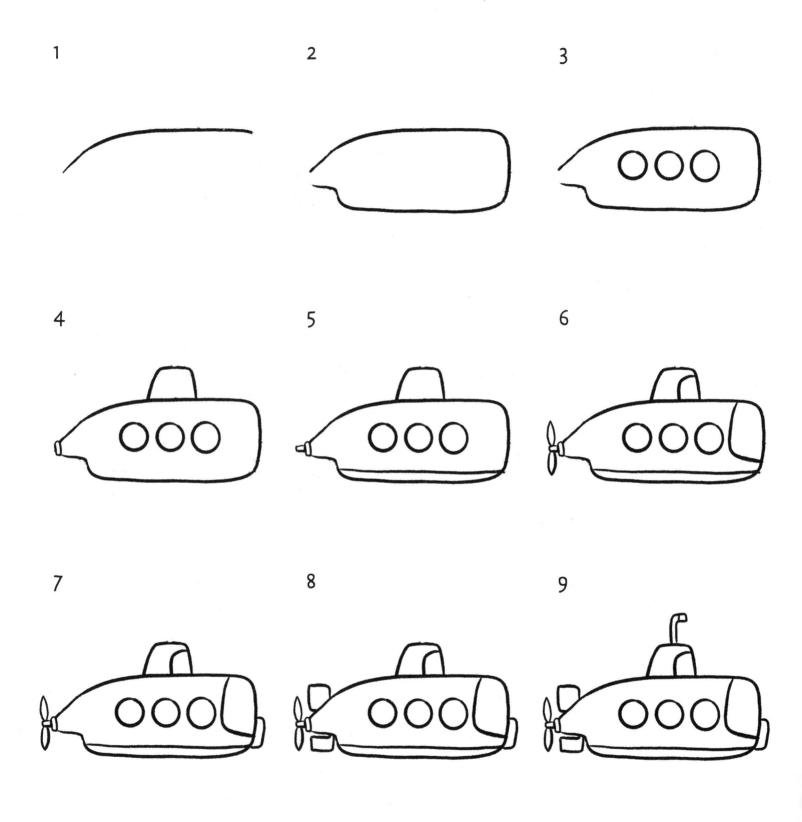

Science in the sea

Submarines like this one have lights and windows for doing research underwater.

Sail away

The tower on top of the submarine is called a sail. It helps to steer the submarine.

Lookout

The sail also has a periscope inside. This lets people inside the submarine see what's happening on the surface of the water.

All About Submarines

* Submarines can be used for exploring the ocean and even for building pipelines underwater.

★ Submarines have very thick walls to protect the people inside and keep them safe.

How to Draw a Skier

1

2

3

4

5

6

7

8

9

Up we go!

A chairlift like this one can carry 4,000 people up the mountain every hour.

Stay safe!

Skiers wear helmets to protect their heads if they fall and goggles to shield their eyes from the wind and sun.

All About Skiing

✳ There are cave paintings of people skiing from 4000 BCE.

⭐ The longest ski jump was 253 m (832 ft). That's 10 lengths of a swimming pool!

How it works

A skier uses their skis to glide over the snow. The poles help them balance and go faster.

How to Draw a Penguin

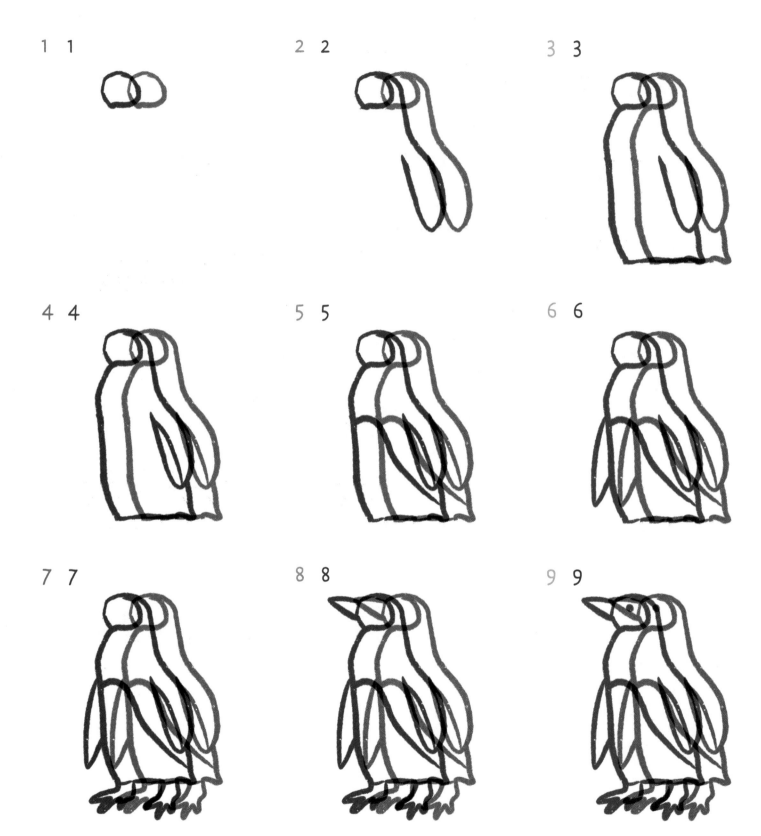

1 1

2 2

3 3

4 4

5 5

6 6

7 7

8 8

9 9

Snow royalty

Emperor penguins like this one are the largest kind of penguins. The smallest type are called fairy penguins.

Antarctic style

Penguins have chubby bodies and waterproof feathers to keep them warm.

Working together

Emperor penguin fathers carry their eggs on their feet to keep them warm while the mother penguins hunt for fish.

All About Penguins

★ There are about 20 different kinds of penguins. In the wild, they only live in the southern hemisphere.

★ Emperor penguins can stay underwater for up to 22 minutes.

How to Draw a Steam Train

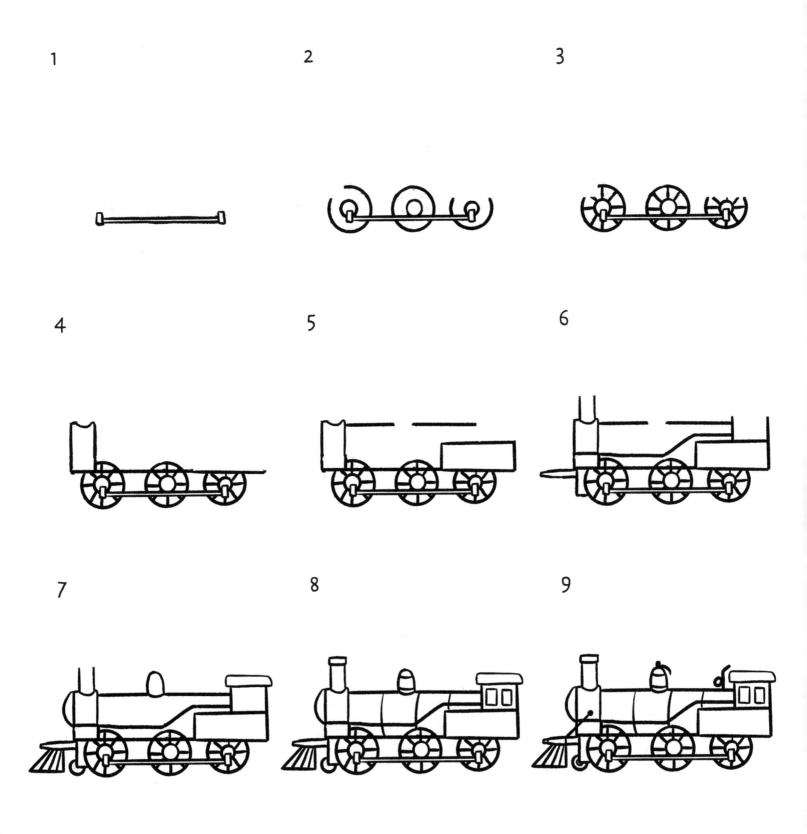

1

2

3

4

5

6

7

8

9

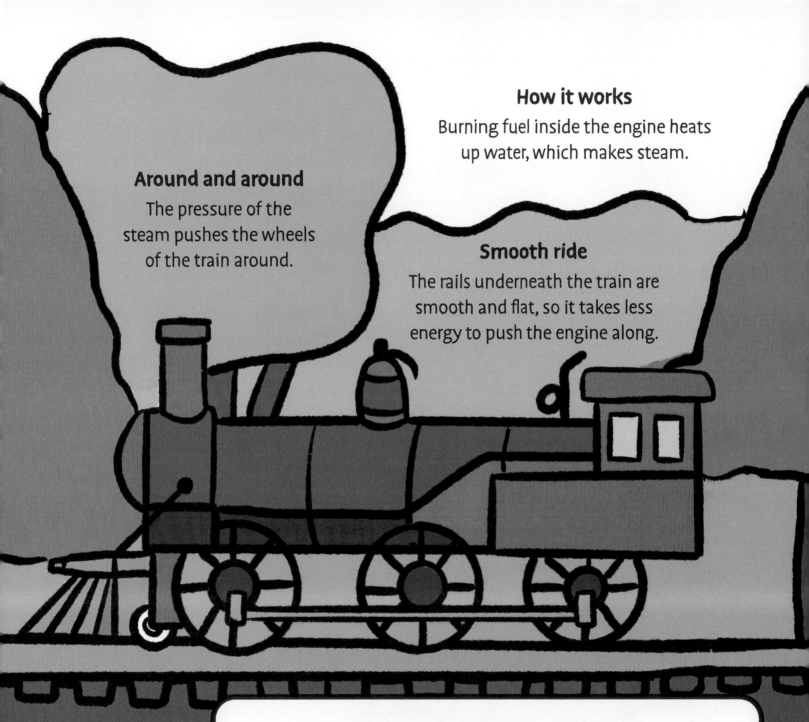

How it works
Burning fuel inside the engine heats up water, which makes steam.

Around and around
The pressure of the steam pushes the wheels of the train around.

Smooth ride
The rails underneath the train are smooth and flat, so it takes less energy to push the engine along.

All About Steam Trains

★ Steam trains were invented 200 years ago. Within a few years, they were being built all over the world.

★ Steam trains are known for their whistling sound. This is made by steam escaping through a whistle.

How to Draw a Builder

1

2

3

4

5

6

7

8

9

86

All About Buildings

★ Concrete is the most popular building material ever. Even the Ancient Romans used it!

★ Other materials used for buildings include wood, mud, bricks, metal, tiles, and glass.

Going up

Scaffolding helps builders reach the high parts of buildings.

Reinforced

Builders wear helmets and steel-toed boots to protect them from accidents on the building site.

How to Draw a Beehive

1

2

3

4

5

6

7

8

9

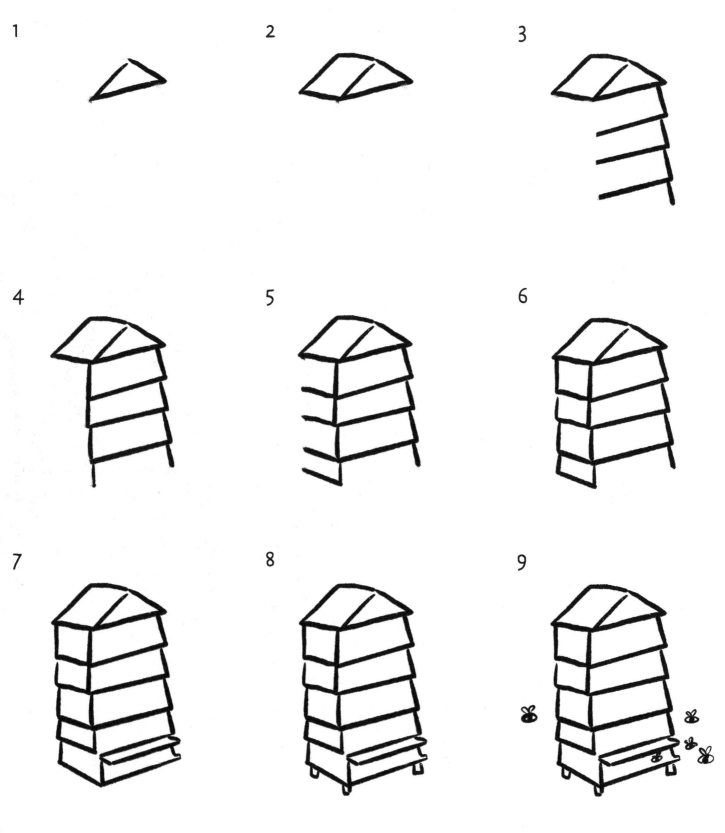

Hive home

A beehive like this one is specially built to make it easier to harvest honey. The beekeeper can lift the top off to collect the honeycomb.

How it works

Bees collect pollen from flowers to make honey in their hive.

Bee bars

There are bars inside the hive to support the honeycomb and keep it in a regular shape.

All About Beehives

* In the wild, bees make their nests in hollow trees or caves instead of hives.

* A beehive can contain up to 60,000 bees—and just one queen.

How to Draw a Llama

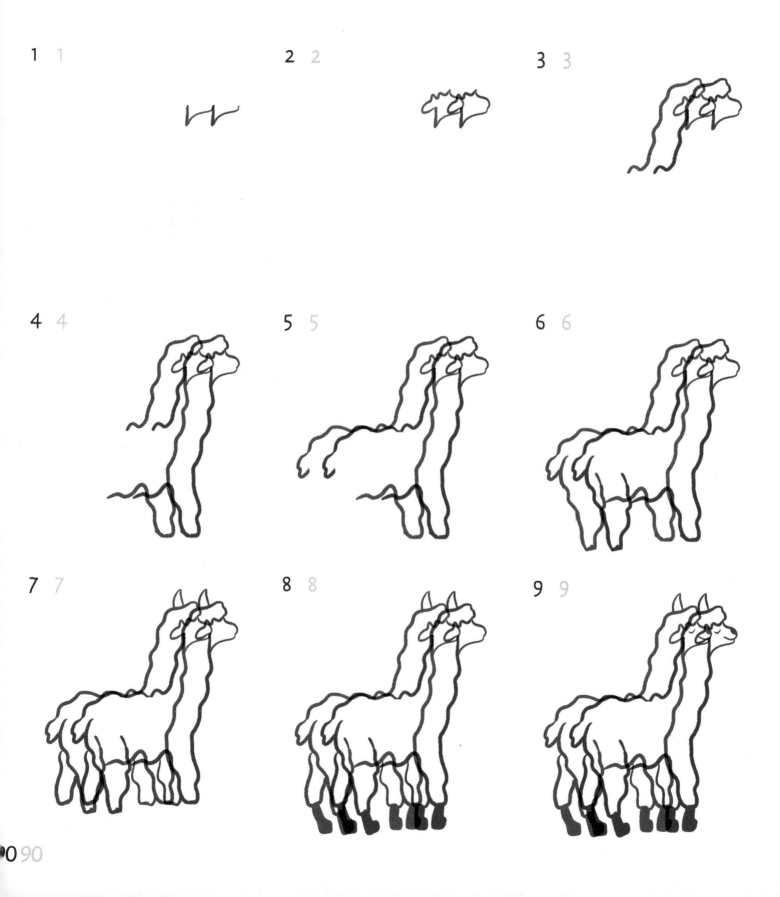

1 1

2 2

3 3

4 4

5 5

6 6

7 7

8 8

9 9

Let's chat!

They communicate by clicking, humming, and gurgling ... and wiggling their ears!

Heavy lifting

Llamas are tough and strong. They can carry heavy weights on their backs.

Llama layers

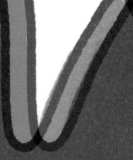

Llamas have two coats of hair: a soft undercoat and a rough outer coat. They can be used to make wool or rope.

All About Llamas

★ Llamas have cloven hooves (two toes on each hoof) to help them walk on rocky mountain paths.

★ Llamas can be used to guard other flocks of alpacas or sheep.

How to Draw a Bus

1
2
3

4
5
6

7
8
9

92

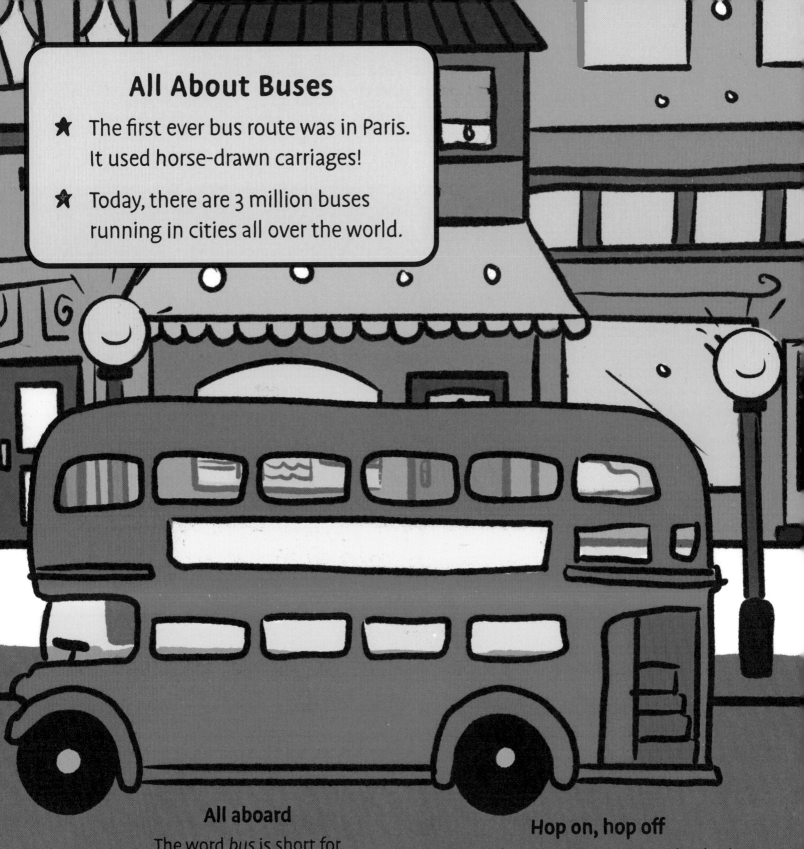

All About Buses

★ The first ever bus route was in Paris. It used horse-drawn carriages!

★ Today, there are 3 million buses running in cities all over the world.

All aboard
The word *bus* is short for "omnibus," which means "for everybody."

Hop on, hop off
Old-fashioned buses in London had a pole on the back, so that people could jump on and off easily.

How to Draw a Chef

1 1

2 2

3 3

4 4

5 5

6 6

7 7

8 8

9 9

Why white?
Chefs wear white to show that they can cook without making a mess!

Whisk it up!
Chefs use a whisk to mix up ingredients smoothly and add air to them.

All About Chefs
★ There are lots of different chefs in a busy restaurant kitchen. Each one has a special job.

★ Chefs have to learn every job in the kitchen before they can become the head chef.

Yes, chef!
Chef is a French word. It means "boss," because the chef runs the kitchen.

Now that you can draw anything ... what will you draw next?

A pirate on a spaceship? A cat on a submarine? A *T. rex* in a hot-air balloon? A knight from the olden days playing the piano or a wizard who goes skiing? You're the artist. You make the rules!